LIVERPOOL
IN A
CITY LIVING

First Published 2004 by Countyvise Limited,
14 Appin Road, Birkenhead, Wirral CH41 9HH

Copyright © 2004 Gerard Fagan

The right of Gerard Fagan to be identified as the author of this work has been asserted by him in accordance with the Copyright, Design and Patents Act 1988.

British Library Cataloguing in Publication Data.
A catalogue record for this book is available from the British Library.

ISBN 1 901231 51 8

DEDICATION

This book is dedicated to my mam and dad, Nora and Joe, Liverpool 3-ites throughout their lives.

Special Thanks to my wife Ann Marie and children Melanie, Melissa and Katy for their assistance, research and above all, patience with me throughout the making of this book.

I would like to express my sincere thanks to the following:

Kay Parrot of the Central Library Records Office and the search room team for their efforts with the supplying of the photographs and the information for use in this book.

Paul Sudbury, a fellow ex Gerard Crescenter for his time and efforts in the supply of photographs and information.

Ron Formby of the Scottie Press for his interest and publicising of my project.

My brother Joe for photographs, inspiration and ideas,

John at Countyvise for his assistance and time taken in the preparation and publication of this book.

Title Page: My dad on the landing, outside 98D Thurlow House.

A LITTLE BIT ABOUT THE AUTHOR

I was born at Mill Road Maternity Hospital on Wednesday 29th August 1962 to Joe and Nora, this making me a Virgo though not a child full of woe. Brother Joe (though not a priest), was, and still is 11 years my senior.

I was brought home to 39 Holly Street, Liverpool 3 where I lived until 1968. With the impending demolition to make way for the new St. Anne Street Police Station, the family moved 200 yards across Christian Street to 98D Thurlow House, part of the Gerard Crescent tenement development.

Outside 39 Holly Street in 1963 with my mam and my older bro, Joey

During this time, I attended Bishop Goss Infants and later Junior School and Saint Joseph's Church in Grosvenor Street, Liverpool 3. I remember Fr. Baker and Fr. Keating as well as some of the teachers such as Miss Keane, Miss Birchall, Miss Brockbank, Miss Thomas, Mr Webster and Headmaster Ted Norton, who incidentally some 40 years earlier had been my dad's teacher there. Unlike nowadays, there wasn't a single car to be found doing the school run, in fact I don't remember more than half a dozen cars in the square at all.

I made many friends during this time and have particularly fond memories of this period and as such cannot imagine life as a kid living anywhere other than the tennys and I'm sure that goes for all the tenny's kids throughout Liverpool. I remember First Holy Communion day was celebrated with a table spread in the 'backie' of Gerard Close at the 'bottom end' as we called it.

St. Joseph's Senior School became disused with the building of the new St. Gregory's Senior School on Prince Edwin Street in the mid

60s. That didn't stop us trying to dodge the caretaker Mr Owen though, in order to enter the building to try and catch a glimpse of the legendary 'cockeyed nun' ghost - never did see it though as it probably never existed!

I remember there were graves down the playground side of the church, the toilets in the schoolyard were demolished to make more space and the metal fire escape which ran up the side of the infants building was also removed. The sloping schoolyard that ran from the back of the Denbigh Castle pub to the gates on Grosvenor Street past the end of St. Joseph's Church was where the footie matches took place.

The problem was when the ball went over into the wasteland behind the Denbigh and it was a case of taking a run and jump and over the wall to retrieve it. Even worse though was when it went over the gates at the bottom of the yard as the ball would continue down Chaucer Street and onto Scotland Road, you were knackered by the time you got back.

I remember it must have been 1971. Decimalisation, and my dad bringing home the new coins and laying them out on the table, the half pence, the new penny and the two pence piece. The five pence, the ten pence and the fifty pence piece had been out a couple of years previously, it was still pound notes then.

The new assembly hall, offices and dinner kitchens were also added in the the late 60s. To the other side of these railings was Kitty Carter's sweetshop, only small but essential, 4 kids fighting for pole position would fill it, and I can almost still see the soft chewy gobstoppers, egg n' milk, fruit salads, blackjacks and mojo's. The building is still there and has been a florists and a sandwich shop since.

Hide n' seek or tick in the playground, and to ascertain who was man it was eachy peachy pear plum or dip, dip, dip my blue ship sailing on the water like a cup and saucer, O-U-T spells out - what was all that about. I remember this was around the time of Slade and T-Rex in the charts, your new car might have been a Ford Capri, Vauxhall Viva, Hillman Imp or Triumph Herald.

Who can forget the chippy teas from Gianelli's on Christian Street, being served by Frank, John or Maria and sitting on the long wooden bench which ran along the back wall aside the white marble table or the brown wooden one next to it. Chips and mushy peas followed by a screwball ice cream in a cone shaped container with a coloured chewy at the bottom.

Over the years and as a visitor to many other tenements where family and friends lived, and getting a bit older now, you begin to grasp the togetherness of the communities built up in these environments. Everyone in the same age bracket seemed to know of or be aware of each other and everyone got on. There were no break-ins and the like as you didn't 'do' your own and your neighbours would have no more than you anyway, but in those days I don't remember anyone 'doing' anyone anyway. I do remember there being a few robbed cars knocking about at one time, coming through the arches between the Gardens and the Crescent until the Corpy put bollards up. It was a short lived affair though and I'm sure brought on by interest in the telly's new cop series the Sweeney.

Being so near to the city centre, weekend pastimes would be trudging round the Walker Art Gallery on William Brown Street where my dad worked and could get me and my mates into the John Moores exhibitions for free. Handy too for seeing the Liverpool team at close quarters when they came home to civic receptions with their trophy haul after winding their way down Scotland Road on an open top bus. The Museum was another local haunt where you eventually got to know every exhibit by heart. Being so close to town meant that when Habitat caught fire and St. Johns Precinct was ablaze, everyone went down there to have a look, the same happened with the Shaky on Fraser street across Islington in 1976. It was great having 'town' as your playground.

Whether playing tick on the 'big steps' which was the Wellington Monument by the fountain or getting down into the 'giants graveyard' which was up Mill Lane at the side of the art gallery, there was always plenty to do.

Shooties in the subway which led under Hunter Street or footie in St. John's Gardens and getting chased by the cocky watchman was another regular event as was the ever welcome 'match in the square'. The square was the name given to the void created by the surrounding blocks of tennys, and the matches often lasted for hours till bad light stopped play, usually ending twenty, nineteen or something like that.

I think this is why people of my generation, brought up like this have no time for the Premiership prima donnas on 40K a week who bemoan playing two matches a week. Another thing they don't have to put up with is kerbstones and having to keep the ball away from Miller's mobiles. These were the mobile van shops that had taken up residence in the square, not very mobile though as all the tyres had gone flat. Very handy for that urgent Bar Six, Pink Panther or packet of Spangles, it wasn't long before a rival mobile appeared in Gerard Gardens, business must have been good.

School lunch times could sometimes be spent going down by Bibby's with some of my class mates who went through a period of trying to catch ringed micks (pigeons with rings on their legs). This was achieved by throwing them corn, waiting for them to get near enough then diving over them with an outstretched coat. I remember reddun's or fantails being of particular interest, I just went along for the adventure. Other lunch pastimes were playing crossfire against my mates and getting so into it that my mam would have to keep reminding us that we'd better get going back to school - 'Aar ey mam.'

With the onset of summer and the inevitable telly coverage of cricket and Wimbledon, the Wembley trophy football would be put into the lobby cupboard for reverse hibernation and out would come the bats and racquets. We're in the days of the chopper and the tomahawk bikes here. The Osmonds and the Jackson Five in the charts and then came that roasting summer of '76 with the bubbling tarmac, endless nights and Eurovision winners, Brotherhood of Man at No.1 and Abba frequent visitors to Top of the Pops. Didn't the six weeks school holidays always seem to shine.

The girl's pastimes were playing gutters either side of the road that ran around the inner perimeter of the square, skipping ropes, hopscotch marked out on the pavement and two balls against the wall on the stairwells at the end of the landing. The stairwells incidentally were painted in 'corpy' cream on the top and green on the bottom,

Holly Street tenements being demolished is the backdrop to this photograph.

Christian Street looking south past the Pontack, library and wash house

separated with a thin black line - Was the Corpy the forerunner to Changing Rooms.

You would awake every morning to the whirring of the milk float, remember this was pre-superstore days. Every Thursday it was the turn of Kirby's coal lorry. Those coalmen must have been fit (that phrase means something else these days doesn't it), up and down four flights of stairs. Staying in bed a little longer on the weekends was a must until ya ma' raked the ashes from last night's coal fire before getting another one going. No setting the central heating to come on at 6am like these days.

Every so often, the gas man or lecky man would arrive, unlock the cash box from the meter, empty the silver onto the table and count out the ten pence pieces into neat £1 rows. After marking the total into his little book, he would then proceed to push a row or two back to my mam as a rebate, must have meant they were overcharging in the first place I thought.

From mid-October and with the nights getting shorter, the next thing on the agenda was stocking up for bonfire night. Old warehouses in Islington and bombdies on Norton Street and Camden Street were prime targets. An army of kids, like ants, invisible beneath doors, making their way back to the square to where they would store them on the flat bit of roof over the stairwell. The bottom enders would store theirs on the flat roof of Jim Moran's shop.

Then the night itself, and didn't it always rain on bommie night! Still, come 7 o'clock the flames were reaching the third landing, sparks filtering out even higher. The distant sounds of the fire engines on their way to put out the bommie in the four squares or up

Scottie Road and the dying embers at half past ten, and wondering what the kids who lived in terraced streets did for theirs.

Next day all there was to show for it was an old bedspring and a load of ashes and the realisation that the footie pitch was now ruined by a massive circle of melted tar.

All the mothers knew each other and would stop for a natter, usually after bumping into one another in the local shops or up Soho Street whilst purchasing the Beano and Dandy from Louis Caplans. Other shops up there were built into the sohoey tenements. There was Cousins, a clothes shop and the fruit and veg shop where the spuds were loose in wooden compartments and you had a metal scoop to shovel them out to be weighed.

In 1977 we moved another 200 yards to 8D Gerard Gardens as this had a third bedroom which was unique as it was directly over the arch above the hod carrier sculpture and had a window looking out towards the pontack on Christian Street and another that looked into the square. It also meant we were a bit nearer to Barneys, which was the sweet shop run by Joan and Peter next to Peppers (the County Hotel) on Islington.

By now my Dad who had worked as a brickie for Halls next to the 'Ponny' (the Pontack) was a foreman for the council having worked his way up from being a porter in such buildings as the Walker Art Gallery, St. George's Hall, Brougham Terrace, Commerce House and the Education buildings in Sir Thomas Street. My brother had also worked for the council in the Central Library, St. George's Hall and Magistrates Court and my mam was a cleaner at the St. George's Hall.

After a short while my dad's job took us down to Blackburn Chambers, the old Blackburn Assurance buildings on the corner of Dale Street and Fontenoy Street. The caretakers flat at 4 Trueman Street was part and parcel of this promotion and so it was with a tinge of sadness but mostly excitement that we moved there just before I left St. Gregory's School.

And so that was the end of my involvement with tenement living, but hey, I was even closer to town now and at just the age I needed to be as I was about to discover lager. I did visit family and friends back in the tenny's though, I mean, they were only ten minutes walk away. In all, that very enjoyable part of my life was over and by the time I moved again, this time to 16 Grosvenor Street in the small block of flats next to where St. Joey's Church was, the tenements had been demolished in the previous couple of years but had obviously left their mark in my memory.

Rather like the school cane and the pump, it was a case of 'they never did me any harm' and as such I have tried to give a general impression of what it was like growing up in that environment. I have called the book 'In a city living' which of course is a play on words of 'Inner city living'

Enjoy the rest.

Gerard Fagan

Outside 98D Thurlow House

IN THE TOWN

WILLIAM BROWN STREET

William Brown Street was a stone's throw from the Gerard Gardens and Gerard Crescent tenement complex's and the local playground for

many of the children growing up in that area at one stage or another in their lives. The close proximity of arguably the finest architectural street in the whole of Liverpool to the once densely populated and slum ridden area off Byrom Street belies belief.

It is the only main thoroughfare in the city to be defunct of shops, residences and public houses though this was not always the case. Originally Shaw's Brow, named after the Shaw family who owned potteries in the street, it had an ample supply of the aforementioned buildings. That all changed when MP William Brown had a large say in the changing face of this well known street.

ST. GEORGE'S HALL:

In 1836 a committee was formed from Liverpool citizens with a view to erecting a building suitable for the performance of secular music. This was due to objections raised about current festivals being held in St. Peter's Church, Church Street. Nearly £25,000 was raised and as at that time assize courts were required in the city, the corporation decided to take over the financing of the building and held a separate competition for the design of each building. Harvey Lonsdale Elmes, only 23 years of age won both competitions detailing a project, which would see both needs covered under the same roof. Elmes was never

to see the work completed, dying only 10 years later, some said from the pressures of his mammoth task. Work was set about on the site of the old infirmary and lunatic asylum in Lime Street. The infirmary, which opened in 1749 but had since been demolished and moved to Brownlow Hill, curiously had a say in the naming of Lime Street. Originally Limekiln Lane, lime kilns stood on what is now the North Western Hotel adjoining Lime Street railway station.

The smells emitted from these caused complaints from the doctors of the infirmary and so they were dismantled and moved north to the Limekiln Lane of today at the top of Burlington Street. The street was thus renamed Lime Street. On 28th June 1838 the foundation stone was laid for the St. George's Hall. Completed and opened in 1854 it has 16 Corinthian columns encasing the main grand entrance which many believe is built back to front. Its main structure and body is built of Derbyshire stone and is one of the finest neo classical buildings in the world having been based on ancient Greece.

THE MUSEUM:

The idea for a city museum was founded in 1850 and originally the Duke Street newsroom built in 1801 served this purpose. Three years

later donations were received and plot of land was earmarked for the construction of the Liverpool City Museum on the north side of Shaw's Brow. MP William Brown (later Sir) provided the money for the building and on 18th October 1860 the Museum was completed and officially opened. The day was made a general public holiday but it was not until exactly one year later with all its exhibits in place that the first public were let through its magnificent doors.

Many extensions and renovations have taken place since. It was destroyed by fire during the May 1941 bombings of WW II. The lower horseshoe gallery did not re-open until 1956 and it wasn't until 8th April 1963 that re-building proper of this fine structure got under way. The occasion was commemorated with a plaque unveiled by the 18th Earl of Derby.

LIVERPOOL CITY LIBRARY:

The Brown Library section was the first to be erected, its foundation stone being laid in 1857 and its opening taking place in 1860. The Picton library, founded by Sir James Allanson Picton (Author, Surveyor and Councillor) was the first purpose built public library in Great Britain. Designed by Cornelius Sherlock, it has 12 Corinthian stone pillars on its semi-circular frontage. Opened in 1879, it was the first public building to have electricity installed. Sir James Picton has a road named in his honour in Wavertree, with a clock tower built in 1884 as a memorial to his wife.

WELLINGTON COLUMN:

This was the next structure to be completed in this area of the city in 1863. It is Liverpool's tallest monument and the only one to contain a spiral staircase. The 15ft high statue of the Duke of Wellington is said to be cast from the guns and cannons captured at the battle of Waterloo. At the base of the columns 'three giant steps' is the board of trades standard measurement table, marked out in iron pegs. The overall height of the structure is 147 feet.

STEBLE FOUNTAIN:

Constructed in 1875, it is named after Colonel R.F. Steble, Liverpool's Mayor of 1874-75 who presented it to the town. The figures around its base represent the four climatic seasons and the fountain itself is operated from the nearby St. George's Hall.

WALKER ART GALLERY:

This building was a gift to the city by brewer and Mayor of Liverpool in 1873, Sir Andrew Barclay Walker. The foundation stone was laid on 28th September 1873 by HRH Duke of Edinburgh on the site of the Townsend Mill in Mill Lane (the lane being still in existence). It was

finally completed and opened on 6th September 1877 by Prince George, later the Duke of Kent. Its opening was also observed as a public holiday, a fine array of buildings now dominating William Brown Street. The pavement was laid out with Yorkshire stone which until recently showed signs of the May blitz with its shrapnel damage.

It was re-laid at about the same time the old tram lines were removed from the street and it was re-cobbled, giving it its present authentic look.

In 1882 Sir Andrew added an extension of five rooms at his own expense. It was renovated and further extended in October 1933 but its most unusual purpose was to come into command six years later when the building was occupied by the Ministry of Food during WW II. It was July 1951 before the gallery re-opened to the public. Apart from the magnificent high ceilings in each room, one of the most striking features are the statues of Michaelangelo and Raphael that guard the entrance. Liverpool artist George Stubbs (1724-1806), a famous horse painter has representations on show in the gallery.

THE COUNTY SESSIONS COURT AND TECHNICAL COLLEGE:

At either end of William Brown Street, both were late comers to the area being built in 1887 and 1901 respectively. However, nothing has been lost in those extra years, their splendour being there for all to see, complementing the earlier buildings. Looking at this street collectively, it is impossible to tell which came first or last. A truly marvellous street with magnificent buildings of incredible architecture.

ST. JOHN'S GARDENS:

This occupies most of the south side of William Brown Street. It was laid out to the rear of St. George's Hall on 29th June 1904 at a cost of £24,000. St. John the Baptist cemetery was originally on this land which was known simply as the heath. This surrounded St. John's Church which was built in 1775. A plaque is sited in the gardens to honour the French Napoleonic prisoners of war who died in Liverpool between 1772 and 1803 and who were buried in the cemetery. Liverpool has an abundance of statues and monuments, seven of which are in St. John's Gardens. Out of Britain's 26 equestrian statues, Liverpool has four.

TRUEMAN STREET

The best surviving 18th century merchant's house in Liverpool c1790. At this time, Dale Street and Water Street were fashionable places to live. The wealthiest shipowners and merchants would live along this stretch until the onset of slum ridden courts saw their mass exodus to outlying parts of the town. Some windows are bricked up to prevent having to pay the daylight tax.

MANCHESTER STREET
KINGSWAY

Manchester Street, Kingsway to give it its full title was laid out in 1821. Prior to this, coaches bound for London and Manchester left via London Road. They first had to proceed from Dale Street negotiating a steep gradient named Shaws Brow (later renamed William

Brown Street). The new route took them via St. Johns Lane and Lime Street (then Lime Kiln Lane). The premises in the middle were once Gilroy & Co. the games shop occupying the bottom corner and Shanks pub, formerly the Tiger is next to the Batch Hatch café. Rose, the owner of the Batch Hatch refused the Council's offer of compensation to relocate and so it is the only survivor in the new development that now forms this side of the street. At the top end of the street near Dale Street stood the Gilmore adult cinema, demolished after an explosion ripped through it.

COMMUTATION ROW

Commutation Row which once housed Britain's first blind school in 1780 here consists of eleven properties, many of them run down and empty. Three public houses, the County (Peppers), the Hare & Hounds and the Court House served the local communities of Gerard

Gardens and Gerard Crescent. The name was given to the street as it was laid out at the time the Commutation Act was being passed in 1836 to prevent the evasion of the window tax by making windows unusually larger than normal.

LONDON ROAD:

Once a thriving mecca with a Woolworths, Co-op and Fine Fare stores. Clothes shops such as Colliers, Burtons, All Mankind and Mailbox, shoe shops such as Clarkes and Londons were all present. Many of the public houses such as the Peppermint Lounge - Sampson and Barlows, Gullivers, the Vancouver, the Tam O'Shanter, The

Swan, The Prince of Wales and The Legs of Man have surrendered to the passing of time. Long established businesses such as T.J. Hughes and the Odeon Cinema (formerly the Paramount) still flourish. A one time photographic studio, Jeromes, was very popular in the area, everyone knows someone who has a photograph from there in their old album.

MUNICIPAL BUILDINGS

These local government offices occupy the entire block between Crosshall Street and Sir Thomas Street, its frontage looking onto Dale Street. It has eighteen statues which encircle the building and a

square pyramid spire which is over 200 feet high. This incorporates a four dial clock tower with a peal of five bells which are rung by the council on special occasions. Built between 1860 and 1866, it opened one year later.

THE TOWN HALL

The original Town Hall built in 1515 was little more than a thatched barn occupying the east side of Juggler Street, now High Street. It was replaced in 1673 by a new hall on the river side of High Street which  survived for almost 80 years. A third hall was designed by John Wood of Bath in 1749 and built on the present site. It was originally only half the size of the present building and was gutted by fire in 1795. It was immediately rebuilt along the same lines but was reconstructed in 1802 by James Wyatt.

The extended front portico was built in 1811 and the council chambers added to the rear of the building in 1900. One of Liverpool's original buildings, though obviously not in its present state, the site is lavished with history. On top of its golden dome sits the statue of Minerva, the Greek god of wisdom. Apart from once being the Lord Mayors mansions and the current council chambers, it is also used for special functions and for entertaining visiting dignitaries. To the rear of the Town Hall is Exchange Flags which houses in its centre, the Nelson Monument. Constructed in memory of the slave trade, this was the first public monument to be erected in Liverpool, the drum originally serving as the ventilation shaft for the bonded warehouses situated below.

The square itself is where merchants gathered to transact business. Indeed buildings still exist in memory of the commodities which were traded. The Corn Exchange in Brunswick Street, The Cotton Exchange in Bixteth Street, The Produce and Fruit Exchanges in Victoria Street are all nearby and, of course, The Stock Exchange in Exchange Flags itself. Sweeting Street opposite the High Street was originally Elbow Lane due to its 'L' shape and is uniquely arched at both ends. This was the first street to have its name inscribed in stone. It takes its name from Alderman Thomas Sweeting who was Liverpool's Mayor in 1698.

THE PIER HEAD'S THREE GRACES

Undoubtedly, one of the most famous skylines in the world. Sailors past and present have recorded that once they see the Liver birds, they know they're in Liverpool. Of the Mersey's 68 mile stretch, this is the gateway being served from the Irish Sea.

THE PORT OF LIVERPOOL BUILDINGS

Completed first of the three in 1907 at a cost of £250,000 it is the long standing home of the Mersey Docks and Harbour Company which owns Liverpool's docks. It has a grand marble and wood interior with a central circular foyer which rises to its 220ft dome. The floor of the foyer has a hand crafted terrazzo marble compass, created by the Italian settlers who lived in the nearby Hunter Street area of the city centre. A grand staircase leads to the floors, which encompass this central tower. The two stone statues at the entrance represent Commerce and Industry.

THE ROYAL LIVER BUILDINGS

The foundation stone was laid on 11th May 1908, the building opening on 19th July 1911. It was built on the filled in George's dock which was named after King George III and was one of the first buildings in the world to use reinforced concrete. Aubrey Thomas was its architect who built the 322ft high structure from grey Aberdeen granite, its purpose, to serve as the headquarters for the Royal Liver Assurance Company.

It has four clock faces, three on the western tower facing north, west and south and one on the eastern tower facing the city. The numbers on the clock are neither figures nor Roman numerals, but simply blocks. In keeping with the King George connection, the clock, named the Great George, which is actually bigger than that of the Houses of Parliament's, was set ticking at the precise moment that King George V was crowned at 1.40pm on 22nd June 1911. On top of the two massive towers are the 18 feet high liver birds, the cormorants, which are the emblem of the City of Liverpool.

THE CUNARD BUILDING

For 125 years, the headquarters of the Cunard Shipping Line. Until its purpose built structure in the Kings Dock area, it was then home to H.M. Customs and Excise which took up the entire ground floor, taking the place of the old Customs House which stood at Canning Place but demolished due to war damage. The smaller of the three buildings, the rest of its floors give way to Company offices, as do the other waterfront buildings. It took three years to build and was completed and opened in 1916.

QUEEN VICTORIA MONUMENT

This site has been the home of four quite contrasting monuments of sorts and is steeped in history. It was recorded that in 1076 Roger of Poictiers built the Liverpool Castle there, hence Castle Street. Evidence does though suggest a later date for its construction. It is known that it was extended between 1235 and 1237 and from it, an underground passage was built leading to the river at the bottom of James Street.

In 1567, the Castle having served for almost five centuries as the watchful eye over the City of

Liverpool, its need as this purpose was now on the wane so in this year the Castle was ordered to house the cattle market. In 1704 the Castle became Liverpool Corporation property and in 1726 was demolished. It was at this time that Lord Derby obtained a grant for the building of a square holding a market on the site of the old Castle site. That site is now named Derby Square.

The market only held stage for a few years and in 1732 St. George's Church was completed and consecrated, the architect being Liverpool's first dock builder and dock master, Thomas Steers. Housing which was facing the church at the top of Harrington Street, Lord Street and Cable Street was demolished in 1827 and St. George's Crescent was laid out and completed two years later. The church itself was demolished in 1899 and the Queen Victoria monument was built between 1902-06 at a cost of £16,000, work commencing just one year after her death.

During the May blitz of 1941, the monument stood alone, untouched as a symbol of hope whilst all around it lay in ruins. At one time a mosaic pattern existed above the encased statue of the Queen, created by the Italian settlers from the nearby Little Italy area of Hunter Street.

CITY CENTRE LIVING:
THE INTER-WAR TENNY'S

During the 1920s and 1930s, Liverpool Corporation entered into a vast rebuilding programme resulting in the removal of insanitary property including slum dwellings and courts, to be replaced by Municipal Tenement buildings or walk up flats. The first phase contained railing style landings whilst a decade later brick wall landings were the fashion. Their forerunners built from 1910 to 1914 just before the 1st World War were already in existence, of course, but these new ones were to be an even greater improvement.

The pre-war maximum height allowance for residential buildings was five storeys so this was the rule of thumb for these new blocks though some were to be only two, three and four storeys high. Many were built in the crowded slum areas that were prolific within a one square mile area of the city centre, the idea being to keep the old communities together in the one place.

GERARD GARDENS/CRESCENT AREA

The Gerard Gardens and Gerard Crescent development also consisted later of Cartwright, Lionel, Downe and Thurlow House together with a block on Christian Street and another smaller block of flats at the extreme opposite end in Hunter Street, named Gerard Close.

Together they contained 398 flats built from 1935 to 1942 after the expansive clearance of a labyrinth of streets that ran eastwards from Byrom Street and northwards from the rear of the great public buildings of William Brown Street. This clearly was poverty existing besides grandeur. The first residents were housed in 1937.

As well as local inhabitants, these streets had housed thousands of Irish emigrants who had fled the 1847 Irish famine and later, Italian settlers who arrived in Liverpool between 1880 and 1912. Both were in search of a better way of life, many originally en route to America but running out of money by the time they had hit Liverpool's central area.

Gerard Street, from which the tenements took their name was named after a local landowner and leading physician who was also a chief magistrate who sat on the council. Such was the population growth just north of the city centre that over a dozen churches and eventually their accompanying schools began to be built. Holy Cross was one such parish, which was sadly demolished in 2003, and St. Joseph's Parish which at one time contained over 10,000 parishoners but which had dwindled to just 1000 by the time dry rot had become irreparable in 1979, forcing demolition.

Sir Lancelot Keay, the architect of Gerard Gardens decided that he wanted to commission a sculpture in his likeness and have it erected above one of the entrances to his jewel in the crown. Residents petitioned for a second sculpture in the form of a hod carrier as one had been killed on site during the construction. Both were undertaken by Herbert Tyson Smith, veteran sculptor of the inscribed foundation stone of the Anglican Cathedral and later, of the bronze carved figures on the St. George's plateau cenotaph war memorial.

The figures for Gerard Gardens were placed over the entrances in Hunter Street and Christian Street. Both of these sculptures can be found on exhibition at the Museum of Liverpool Life at Mann Island. A cast replica takes pride of place at the end of the present Christian Street, where, together with its plinth, commemorate all of those killed during construction work as well as the residents of Gerard Gardens from 1937 to 1987.

Gerard Gardens and the mid section of Gerard Crescent were completed in 1937 whilst the demolition of streets running westwards towards Byrom Street was still ongoing. During 1938 and 1939 the four blocks of Cartwright (complete with corner shop known locally during the 1970s as Jim Moran's), Lionel, Downe and Thurlow House began to spring up in that order taking their names from the streets which were being cleared to make way for them.

It was as late as 1942 before the remainder of Hunter Street was cleared and the continuation of Gerard Crescent was commenced to

Hunter Street at its south end and Christian Street to the east. The enclosure was completed with a smaller three storey block on Hunter Street called Gerard Close. This block was smaller than the rest of the square because by then, the council policies had changed to building this type of accommodation, tenements now being old-hat.

Christian Street was named after local potter Philip Christian who had a dwelling built on land there made from salvaged materials from the nearby square tower structure called Gibson's folly. Other local landmarks on Christian Street were Liverpool's circus theatre which gave rise to the aptly named nearby Circus Street. A saw mill and wash house existed between Christian Street and Clare Street and from the Islington end of Christian Street stood the Wellington pub, known to locals as Cassons but not to be confused with the Wellington which still stands today on St. Anne Street, albeit derelict.

John and Frank Gianelli's famous fish and chip shop stood near the top of Hunter Street, facing which was the Transport and General Workers Union building which was on the next block to St. Anne's School. Across Springfield Street, known locally as Springy was another public house, the Pontack, which also served the local community and from the 40s through to the 90s notable licensee's were Don Coutts, Peggy Gaskell and Charlie Pepper. To the south of the Pontack across Pontack Lane was the public library, to its north, Hall and Sons, builders, and McArdles Chandlers shop to name but a few.

The tenement flats originally contained a coal fire in the living room with another in the larger bedroom and had the luxury of electricity and an indoor bathroom. Such splendour was that each landing flat also had a back veranda. Families moving into these tenement blocks were long used to washing in a tin bath in front of an open fire, open fire cooking, an outside toilet, gaslight, and in many cases a communal tap in the courtyard serving many families.

From 1950, with changing Council policies, lifts were installed in the Gardens, Crescent and all the larger blocks throughout Liverpool, though it was less than twenty years before most of these were disused. In the mid 1970s the corporation undertook a mass modernisation programme of its tenement stock and Old Swan company Robinson Willey supplied the corporation with gas fires to be fitted in the living room. In the summer of 1977 the whole of the Gerard Gardens/Crescent complex underwent a total re-roof.

In the 1980s and with the expansion and widening of the inner ring road to cater for more traffic moving in and out of the city centre, plans were abound to widen Hunter Street to join the recently created New Islington at its east end. It was decided to re-house the residents of the Gardens and the Crescent. The City bound and outbound flyovers of Churchill Way had already been up and running for over a decade existing alongside the blocks and they had also survived the Kingsway Tunnel approach road scheme whereas others had not. However, some of the community have remained in the area in the new build modern housing in the newly laid Gerard Street, Tom Mann Close, St. Joseph's Crescent and the existing Christian Street. The Pontack is the only landmark that remains from when the tenements existed, though it is no longer a pub.

1937 - The demolition of the Hunter Street and Gerard Street area for the redevelopment to include Cartwright, Lionel, Downe and Thurlow House. The main spire shown is that of St. Stephen's Church whilst in the distance to the far left is the Blackburn Assurance Building and to the right, the spire of Holy Cross Church.

1937 - Gerard Gardens can be seen here behind the fine buildings of William Brown Street. To their west lies a labyrinth of streets waiting to be cleared. Gerard Crescent has only the mid section completed. Across the strong lines of Byrom Street, running north, you can make out the beginnings of Fontenoy Gardens. East of Gerard Gardens are the impressive four squares on Soho Street.

1938 - Cartwright, Lionel and Downe House have now been added west of Gerard Gardens. The fourth block, Thurlow House was added a year later. Beyond them, the front blocks of Fontenoy Gardens are being built, complete with canopy overhead the shops below.

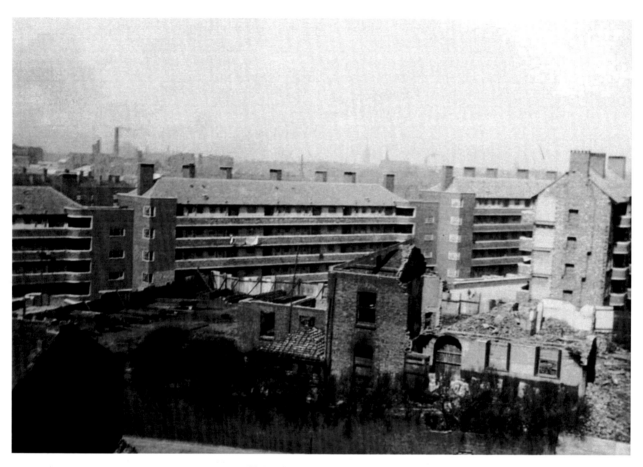

1942 - Taken from the back of the Walker Art Gallery roof. Hunter Street north side is under demolition to allow the continuation of Gerard Crescent and the building of Gerard Close. Lionel House is flanked by Cartwright and Downe House.

1958 - Gerard Gardens and Gerard Crescent complex is now well completed, so too is Fontenoy Gardens. In between, the new technical college is being built but St. Stephen's Church, Byrom Hall, the Army & Navy stores and the Dunbar Castle pub are still there awaiting demolition for the widening of Byrom Street.

1937 - Gerard Gardens, Through the arch, Christ Church School on Christian Street can be seen.

The rear of Thurlow House clearly showing the labyrinth of streets such as Thurlow Street, Downe Street and Kilin Street which have been cleared ready for building of the new technical college. The picture is taken from a derelict property in Circus Street. In the background can be seen Holly Street landing dwellings and tenements beyond the Myrtle public house.

Gerard Close: The last piece in the jigsaw, completed only in 1952 when the council policy was moving towards these three storey blocks.

1966 - Hunter Street/ Christian Street junction showing Gerard Gardens.

1966 - Hunter Street looking towards Byrom Street. The buildings seen here were to make way for the flyover.

1966 - The L1 Ribble bus, having left Skelhorne Street depot is en route to Crosby. On the left is St. Anne's School, next to it is the Transport and General Workers Union building. On the right is Gianelli's fish and chip shop and Wellington pub. Across Islington is the Gaumont picture house in Camden Street.

1966 - Byrom Street east side at the bottom of Hunter Street showing the technical college and the back of Cartwright and Lionel House.

1969 - The newly opened eastbound flyover, the westbound carriageway being still under construction. The Bullring is top right, Gerard Gardens/Crescent is middle left facing the technical college on Byrom Street is Fontenoy Gardens. Bispham House and Adlington House hi-rise flats are newly completed and Standish Street 'coffin blocks' stand between Fontenoy Street and Marybone, as does Holy Cross Church.

Taken from under the flyover across Hunter Street in 1985.
This is the first stage of the demolition to allow the widening of the aforementioned street.

Seen from the John Moores University car park. One time local shop Jim Moran's, later owned by the Miller family, is razed to the ground. The side of Gerard Close can now be clearly seen.

Looking up the 'backie' which ran the length of the four blocks. The original wall of the square which ran up the brew is still in place today, Tom Mann Close is now built to the east of it.

The iron ball moves in. 'The violent playground thirty years on' graffiti refers to the film that was shot there in 1957 starring Stanley Baker and Anne Heywood. Also featured were Peter Cushing and a young David McCallum, Freddie Starr and Melvin Hayes.

The hod carrier sculpture which once adorned Gerard Gardens, now found in the Museum of Liverpool Life.

The architect sculpture which once adorned Gerard Gardens, now found in the Musuem of Liverpool Life.

The replica statue, dedicated to those who lost their lives in the construction industry. Its plinth is dedicated to the former residents of Gerard Gardens from 1937 to 87

Islington/Fraser Street junction just prior to demolition

Fraser Street looking towards Islington with property in danger of collapse

1990 - Fraser Street at its junction with London Road showing Gullivers Bar, renamed Trophys

Christian Street: bungalows now flank the Pontack pub (Ponny) where once stood Hall's the builders and the Junior Library

Comus Street. Some of the flats in this style have already bit the dust, these will follow shortly.

Grosvenor Street in the old St. Joseph's Parish, earmarked for demolition.

The Old Haymarket. St. John's House stands alone on St. John's Lane before the Queens Square regeneration programme. A hotel and multi storey car park now accompany the building. Buses are using this area as their terminus.

The demise of the Holy Cross Church in December 2003.

SCOTLAND ROAD:

Fontenoy Gardens, built between 1935 and 1940 fronted onto Byrom Street incorporating shops and offices into their ground floor level. The careers office took up residence under one block near Great Crosshall Street as did the housing lettings office. Nearby, jewellers, Stanleys could be found whilst at the Addison Street end there was Sykes Cash Stores which became Scott's grocery/mini-market shop.

Fontenoy Gardens from the roof of Blackburn Assurance Buildings on Dale Street. Arden House hostel can be seen in the distance over the rooftops.

Between these, John Harpers which became a fruit and veg shop and then a fish and chip shop and then further along near to the railway tunnel, a long standing tenant of one shop who remained until the closure of the block was Lawrence's newsagents. To the other side of Addison Street stood Melia's, Scotland Road post office, Roberts & Bromleys and further north, the Gaiety picture house. The blocks were separated by the deep tunnel cut of the now disused Waterloo dock goods railway which ran under Byrom Street and up to Edge Hill station.

Fontenoy Street is the only street in Liverpool to take its name from a battle in which the British lost (1745), Addison Street however started life in much grimmer circumstances. Originally known as Sickmans Lane and Deadmans Lane, it was where 200 dead were buried after falling victim to the black plague which hit Liverpool in 1651, many of these terminally ill people were housed in cabins there. Joshua Rose who himself had nearby Rose Place, Rose Hill and Rose Vale named after him, gave grand names to the streets north of Fontenoy Gardens taking their names from poets and poems. These being Addison, Milton, Edgar, Alexander Pope, Chaucer, Cavendish, Ben Johnson, Virgil, Dryden and Juvenal Streets.

1951 - Byrom Street property being demolished to make way for the continued building of Fontenoy Gardens.

1939 - Fontenoy Gardens from the junction of Byrom Street and Addison Street showing the corner shop Syke's (which became Scotts) and a little further along, John Harpers.

1966 - Byrom Street looking northwards from near the Queensway tunnel entrance across the junction with Great Crosshall Street.

1967 - Looking down Richmond Row. The new technical college is on the left and Berry's pawn shop at No. 53 is present. On Byrom Street is Fontenoy Gardens, behind them, Bispham and Adlington House are under construction. The small row of property north of Addison Street are Melia's, the post office and Roberts & Bromleys.

Byrom Street: Fontenoy Gardens once stood either side of the disused railway tunnel giving good views to the prams, bike frames, mattresses and other junk dumped down there towards the latter years.

Fontenoy Street today where oncr stood Fontenoy Gardens. Six bungalows seen here use land which once housed a block containing 40 flats. The tenements were an innovation in space saving techniques and communities were born out of them.

Further north is St. Anthony's Parish, another area whose population increased dramatically due to the influx of Irish emigrants from the aforementioned famine of 1847 when 120,000 Irish sailed to Liverpool in any craft they could find. Sadly, many were to die of illness and disease and over 2,300 are buried in the grounds and the crypt of St. Anthony's Church which was established in 1804.

By the turn of the century it was decided to rid this area of its slums and courts and it was a massive operation which was to run into the 1930s. Many landing dwellings were built just before the 1st world war as a forerunner to the tenements. Just over twenty years later, Ashfield, Woodstock and Hopwood Gardens were built on the west side of Scotland Road to alleviate much of the hardship, the blocks serving their purpose for less than fifty years before they were demolished in 1983. The communities of Scotland Road were gradually broken up starting in 1969 with the demolition of much of the south end of the road to accommodate the Kingsway Tunnel approach roads. Literally dozens of public houses were lost in this and more recent 'improvements' as they were bulldozed to the ground.

To the opposite side of Scotland Road was the smaller development of Wilbraham House on Wilbraham Street, whose site when demolished lay as wasteland for many years. Heading back towards the city centre beyond Collingwood Street were Lawrence Gardens which stood on Lawrence Street facing St. Martins Market, known to all as Paddy's Market. This was situated on Cazneau Street and Juvenal Street. This development too was the victim of the Kingsway Tunnel, finding itself isolated by the circular approach road which cut a swathe across Horatio Street and Gt Nelson Street. The blocks were

Virgil Street looking towards Great Homer Street - 1990.

built in 1931 and demolished in the early 1970s. Nearby, built in 1885 but demolished in 1966 were the Victoria Square dwellings. These were five blocks, each with five storeys having 269 flats ranging from a single room to three bedrooms, twelve shops were also built into the street level. In 1941, one of the blocks was severely damaged in the blitz and later demolished. Juvenal Buildings which stood on the south side of Juvenal Street from 1890 did not even last as long as that.

1969 - The Kingsway Tunnel approach roads are under construction resulting in the devastation of the bottom end of Scotland Road. Top left are the four squares, top right, Gerard Gardens/Crescent. In the middle, left in total isolation are Lawrence Gardens, facing these is the old St. Martin's Market on Cazneau Street.

Silvester Street junction with St. Augustine Street showing the tenements and the three storey high blocks.

VAUXHALL ROAD:

Vauxhall Gardens: Once thriving with the spontaneous football matches but nearing the end of its life span and being used as a car park by the nearby college students

To the west of Fontenoy Gardens across Vauxhall Road were Vauxhall Gardens which also consisted of blocks on Highfield Street and Westmoreland Place. These were demolished in the 1990's. This community was served by both Holy Cross Parish and St. Mary's, Highfield street. Both of these churches have now been demolished, Holy cross just recently in 2003 after both having the distinction of originally being blitzed in 1941 and then rebuilt. St. Mary's was the first Catholic church in Liverpool after the reformation, Holy Cross was built originally to cater for the Irish famine victims and ever expanding population in that area of the city centre.

Looking up Highfield Street towards Pownall Square which was a market square until the late 1880s and named after William Pownall, Liverpool's mayor of 1767. The Rose and Crown, then managed by

local character Terry McHale and the Wedding House managed by Alf and Alice were integral to the local community. A mile further north can be seen the three ugly sisters, a local name for the trio of chimneys of Clarence Dock power station which was opened on October 18th 1938.

The Cross Keys on the corner of Earle Street and Prussia Street and the St. Pauls on the square of the same name were local to Vauxhall Gardens.

1966 - Taken from the top of the Municipal Buildings on Dale Street. Vauxhall Gardens and Highfield Street are in view. Industry in the background from left to right are Bibby's, Clarence dock power station, Stanley Dock tobacco warehouse (now the Sunday Heritage market) and Tate & Lyle sugar refinery.

Blackstock Gardens on Blackstock Street were completed in 1934 with an in-built corner shop which was a feature of some of these tenement blocks. Consisting of 134 flats, another feature was a centre court complete with ornamental gates and stone pots which fronted onto Paul Street. Nearly one hundred locals were killed in this area in December 1940 and whole residential areas left in ruins after Luftwaffe air-raids, such was this area's close proximity to the docks. A memorial to those killed stands on Vauxhall Road, near Carruthers Street.

Beyond these flats to the north were a number of developments from different eras. These were primarily on Burlington Street and consisted of flats from the 1920s on the south side, some of which incorporated shops and a doctor's surgery on their ground floor level. These were demolished in 1989. Facing were Portland Gardens from the 1930s, and some fifty years later these were cleverly converted into low density housing and sheltered accommodation for the elderly after the Portland Housing Co-operative was set up in 1978 to try and save these blocks.

Eldon Street - just weeks before the iron ball paid a visit, the residents long since gone but not the community as the Eldonian Co-operative Association is born out of this area.

Part of this area consisted of blocks in Eldon Street, the residents of which took matters into their own hands when it became apparent their community was to be dispersed to suburban areas of the city like so many before them. Under the guidance of Tony McGann and with government aid, the Eldonian Housing Co-operative was formed and they entered into negotiations with the Merseyside Development Corporation who owned much of the land that was to be used. Their venture was rewarded in the early 1990s with a fantastic modern housing development running alongside the Liverpool to Leeds canal.

The Eldonian Village now consists of a community centre, sports centre, sheltered accommodation and village hall for functions and social events.

The communities of Burlington Street and Vauxhall Road were heavily reliant on large employers in the area who had historically employed generations of the same families, such as the Docks, Tillotsons, British American Tobacco (the BA) and sugar refiners Tate

& Lyle and Fairries. Dock work diminished greatly in the 1970s and 80's with the opening of the Seaforth Container terminal and the subsequent switch from conventional cargo to containerised movements. With the closure of industry along the river side of Vauxhall Road, many families were left out of work whilst others moved out of the area to seek employment.

Burroughs Gardens at its junction with Limekiln Lane in 1990. Kingsway Court Apartments, built by Wimpey in 1992 now stand here

Portland Gardens - Revamped into sheltered accommodation

Eldon Grove. Built 1912, dilapidated in the 1990s but undergoing restoration to its former glory in 2004. New tudor style housing will be built in its shadow to complement this block.

A model of Eldon Grove and Bevington Street showing how it looked in its heyday around 1914 when newly built.

1969 - An aerial view looking from the Vauxhall area, eastwards to Netherfield Road. Vauxhall Gardens is to the extreme right, Blackstock Street blocks in the centre of the picture and Eldon Street, Burlington Street and Portland Gardens to the left. Across Scotland Road stands Lawrence Gardens isolated by the surrounds of the Kingsway tunnel approach road. Further up Scotland Road to the left are Wilbraham House on the east side and Woodstock and Ashfield Gardens facing St. Anthony's Church. There are over twenty hi-rise flats in view in the Netherfield Road district from Corinth Tower on the extreme left to the piggeries on the right.

ST. ANNE STREET:

To the north of Islington and running east of St Anne Street stood what were known locally as the four squares, dating from 1935, its layout being self-explanatory. Bordered by Springfield Street, Harker Street, Wakefield Street, Mansfield Street but mainly on Soho Street, at its four corners stood the parishes of St. Francis Xaviers, Salisbury Street, Holy Trinity, Springfield Street, St. Anne's, St. Anne Street and St. Mary of the Angels (the Friary), Fox Street.

Most of the development lay just behind Letherens woodworks on St. Anne Street, other industry in the area were Jaem joiners, Hertz truck hire, W.H. Snow decorators and Pitt & Scott textiles distributors. The tenement blocks fronting onto Soho Street incorporated a small row of shops which changed hands frequently during the 1960s and 70s. Other local shops in the immediate area were Joe Levines, Joe Vermigglio's, Morris's grocers and newsagents which, still trading has now expanded to a post office and off licence and Austin's fish and chip shop. Caplans tobacconists on the corner of William Henry Street was around the corner from Peppers betting shop and the rag and bone yard and was owned by Louis Caplan, an ex Lord Mayor of Liverpool. The four squares were demolished in 1977, the site now being mainly landscaped with the local community moving to new modern housing to the opposite side of Soho Street and either side of William Henry Street.

Soho Street/William Henry Street junction viewed from where once stood Birkett Street tenements.

1966 - Springfield Street. The sweet shop sandwiched by the lodging houses became Manny Charles betting shop. To the right is the Holy Trinity church perimeter wall and beyond the four squares on Soho Street is Foster's supply Co. The spire of SFX church is in the background.

1967 - Soho Street looking north from its east side. Is that you in the car?
The shops under the tenements can just be seen.

1966 - Soho Street looking north from its west side.

1966 - William Henry Sreet looking towards Langsdale Street. The Great Eastern pub is on the corner. Was that your car?

1966 - St. Anne Street at its junction with Islington. Holy Trinity church, which was destroyed by fire in the 1970s can be seen above the block which was shortly to be demolished.

Fox Street showing the friary church and old dilapidated property soon to be demolished.

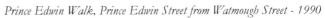

Prince Edwin Walk, Prince Edwin Street from Watmough Street - 1990

Shaw Street, west side from the top of William Henry Street - 1990

Shaw Street looking south nearer to its Islington end.

Shaw Street looking across Islington towards Moss Street. Office World now stands here.

Great Richmond Street dwellings: A lone Mini Cooper signifies one of the last remaining residents.

Great Richmond Street dwellings: Renovated and enjoying a new lease of life.

Just north of these blocks on the other side of Mansfield Street and running parallel with Birkett Street stood a number of separate blocks built in 1937 all served by their own stairwell. Birkett Street blocks were built just east of the site of the old open air baths. Local industry in nearby Richmond Row included Armstrong Tarry, Thomas Bell, Frank Whites, Wiggins Teape and Full Swing. The continuation of Richmond Row, Everton Brow, had a row of shops that backed onto the Friary consisting of Railtons tobacconist (known as Railo's), Joe Mitchells workshop and Kits fish and chip shop. Kit also owned and lived above the Ah Tai launderette on Soho Street which stood next door to Lenny Cotters barbers, famed for his basin head haircuts. Keisers clock tower, a landmark still in existence today, which stands on the corner of St. Anne Street and Birkett Street was part of the Rushworth and Drapers piano stores who had their shops in Whitechapel and Islington.

On the corner of St. Anne Street and Gt. Richmond Street, to the north of the four squares and the Birkett Street blocks still stand Gt. Richmond Street dwellings, preserved as only one of their kind. Affectionately known locally as ghost town due to the lack of activity there because of its older residents (and it only consisted of 20 flats), it was sold off and re-developed as private flats in the 1990s and renamed St Anne's apartments. An archway that was originally one of the three entrances to this small 'L' shaped block was cleverly incorporated as an additional room to one of the flats within the complex.

1966 - The junction of St. Anne Street and Richmond Row. The St. Anne pub is in the foreground and beyond Great Richmond Street tenement dwelling is St. Anne's church from which St. Anne Street derives its name.

Holly Street ran west from St. Anne Street down to Christian Street. To its north side were mock tudor landing blocks which formed a square by running along Christian Street, back up Birkett Street and along St. Anne Street to complete the block. The St. Anne Street block of this square contained shops at ground level and a 'backie' or inner courtyard was formed merely by its shape. These were similar to

1966 - Holly Street (abolished) seen from Christian Street. landing dwellings on the left from 1912 and tenements on the right from 1923. There's a lorry coming out of Gaskell's potato merchants and beyond St. Annes Street is the Royal Standard pub known as Kings. Further up William Henry Street are the Piggeries.

Eldon Grove and many of the landing dwellings in the Burlington Street and Scotland Road area which were built in the decade just before the 1st World War and were forerunners to the tenements.

To the south side of Holly Street stood tenements with railing landings dating from 1923. At the top of the street stood Gaskell's potato merchants and at the bottom, across Myrtle view stood the Myrtle public house, taking its name from the old name for the street which was Myrtle Street. These tenements varied in height with the slope of the street and as such, a few of the lower level flats at the top end of the street were actually below ground level and were reached by means of steps down to the front door.

1966 - The front of Holly Street tenements from Christian Street. The back of the Myrtle pub can be seen in the fore ground. In the distance the side of Gaskell's.

Holly Street was demolished in its entirety in 1969 to make way for St. Anne Street police headquarters which was built to replace the old Rose Hill Bridewell which stood almost facing.

KIRKDALE AND EVERTON:

Kirkdale tenements known locally as 'the buildings' were among some of the first built, utilising the land of the former Owens timber yard in Liverpool 4. Four blocks were erected in the mid 1920s, namely Owen, Melrose, Stanley and Fonthill House to mirror the names of existing local roads.

1966 - Looking along Rose Hill. The police station is on the right, the side view being Peover Street. Extreme left is McDougall's funeral parlour, Birkett Street landing dwellings are facing.

A unique feature on this development was an ornate clock at the second floor level on one of the blocks. Modern housing now covers this area with only a fraction of the old community remaining.

On St. Domingo Road stood Sir Thomas White Gardens. A claim to fame is that Paul McCartney lived at a ground floor flat here with his family as a four year old, albeit only for a few months. These tenements were demolished in 1984.

THE BULLRING:

St. Andrews Gardens, Copperas Hill were opened in 1935. Its nickname, the bullring or bully is derived from its semi-circular shape which it was given in remembrance of the lands former use when

The Bullring - St. Andrews Gardens seen from within and from Copperas Hill

bulls were driven through Bronte Street to Trowbridge Street slaughter house in the 1840s. Some of these blocks at St. Andrews Street were separated by the deep tunnel cut of the railway lines serving Lime Street station.

Similarly to Myrtle Gardens, these were given listed status as a fine example of tenement living and have now been modernised by Riverside Housing for student accommodation.

1969 - An aerial view of the Bullring, The Metropolitan Cathedral of Christ the King and the tenement complexes beyond.

Seymour Street: Dilapidated terracing which has since been rejuvenated to its former glory.

Lord Nelson Street: Bedsit land could do with the same TLC afforded to nearby Seymour Street

St. Andrews Gardens. - Could this not have been done with some of the other tenement developments?

THE SOUTH END:

The tenements of Edge Hill, Toxteth, the Dingle and Chinatown surround a number of streets of character in the South end of Liverpool.

Huskisson Street is named after William Huskisson MP, who was killed by George Stephenson's Rocket on the opening day of the

Liverpool to Manchester railway on 15th September 1830. In his eagerness to meet and shake the hand of the Duke of Wellington who had come up from London for the occasion, he inadvertently stepped onto the rails and was mowed down forthwith. It happened at Parkside, Golborne on what were the Rainhill trials section of the railway. Edge Hill station, built by Stephenson, was opened

Dusk over Huskisson Street. It could almost be a London scene from Jack the Ripper.

earlier that day. Injured, Huskisson was transported on the 'Northumbrian' to Eccles vicarage where he died at 9pm the same night.

He made history, though not in the way he would have wanted to, being the first man to be killed by a train, on the very first opening day. The Rocket went on to win the trials. Huskisson was buried at St. James cemetery on 24th September 1830 and the large Huskisson mausoleum is situated in the centre of the grounds to this day, though the statue of him that was inside has been removed for safe keeping. By the end of the 18th century a larger network of streets were developing outwards from the city centre, particularly to the south. Toxteth and Edge Hill were yet to be developed as we know them today but West Derby, Kirkdale and Everton to the north were then but villages.

RODNEY STREET:

Splendid period property complete with elegant balconies and mock gas lamps. This is Liverpool's equivalent to London's Harley Street with many doctors and specialists taking up residence for their

practices here. The street was built between 1785 and 1820. It was named after Admiral George Brydges, 1st Baron Rodney (1718-1792). He became a peer after leading a battle in St. Lucia where he defeated the French. It is also the birthplace and one time residence of many famous people. Lytton Strachey, the biographer lived at No.80. Nicholas Monsarrat, author of the 'Cruel Sea' was born at No.11 in 1910. Beatles manager and entrepreneur Brian Epstein was born at No. 4 and also born here was poet, Arthur Hugh Clough (1819-1861). His daughter, Annie Clough, born at No.74 became the first principal of Newsham College, Cambridge. Ambrose Dawson MD, a world renowned specialist was the first man to reside here. Perhaps Rodney Street's most famous son was William Ewart Gladstone born on 29th December 1809 at No. 62. He was Liberal Prime Minister 1868-74, 1880-86 and 1892-94. His renown extends to a street, public house and a statue in his honour located in St. John's Gardens. He died on 19th May 1898 and is buried in Westminster Abbey. St. Andrews Church of Scotland with its pyramid tomb of John McKenzie is also a feature of this street.

PRINCES BOULEVARD:

In the Bohemian area of Liverpool 8. This has two carriageways, each with a separate name. Princes Road runs North to the city centre. Princes Avenue on the other hand runs South towards Liverpool's first public park, Princes Park from which the Avenue derives its name, it having been laid out for easier access to the park. The Boulevard was

redeveloped to its present standing in the 1870s, flanked either side by four and five storey residences, many now converted into flats. The park itself which is situated just north of Liverpool's largest, Sefton Park, covers 40 acres of Toxteth land and was given to the city by Richard Vaughan Yates in 1843.

ABERCROMBY SQUARE:

Is named in honour of General Sir Ralph Abercromby (1734-1801) who was commander of the British Army in Egypt. He was killed in action in the battle of Alexandria.

CANNING STREET:

Named in honour of George Canning, four times Liverpool MP in 1812, 1816, 1818 and 1820 and PM in 1827. He died in office as Governor of India.

CATHERINE STREET:

Runs South from Myrtle Street to Princes Road and was given the name by builder and architect William Jones (1788-1876) in memory of his mother. It was then known as the Bloomsbury area when he constructed many houses, his own being No. 35 where he lived until his death.

FALKNER STREET:

Formerly Crabtree Lane was named after local resident Edward Falkner. He managed to enrol 1000 men in an hour to defend Liverpool against a threatened French invasion in 1797. The Square of the same name was later laid out by him under the name Wellington Square. It acquired the nickname Falkners folly as it was so far out of town. It is now the more appropriate Falkner Square.

UPPER STANHOPE STREET:

Along Blair Street towards the Anglican Cathedral you can see the rear of some of the derelict buildings whose frontage looked out onto Upper Parliament Street.

THE ANGLICAN CATHEDRAL:

Looking down at this magnificent building across Cathedral Gardens from the vantage point of Hope Street, you can almost hear the echo of choristic voices in the autumn wind. Pure architectural genius greets your eyes from every angle. Built from dark pink sandstone quarried locally, the foundation stone was laid on 19th July 1904 by Edward VII. The designer was a Catholic, Giles Gilbert Scott, then only 21 years of age. He supervised the building of the Cathedral for 56 years until his death in 1960 and was knighted by King George V at Knowsley Hall prior to his death.

The completion of the building was undertaken by Frederick Thomas. Buried under the foundation stone is political literature of the day, interesting reading today I'm sure. The Lady Chapel was the first portion to be completed in 1910 but it took two world wars to slow its steady progress. A feature of the construction was that once a portion was started, it was completed down to its finest detail before the next part was commenced. In 1924 it was partly consecrated at the eastern section in the presence of King George V and Queen Mary but it was not until 25th October 1978 that it was officially completed and consecrated with Queen Elizabeth II in attendance.

Built on St. James Mount which was originally a pleasure ground called Mount Zion, it has a fantastic array of record breaking architecture and features. It contains the biggest Gothic arches ever built, the largest Gothic vaults in the world, has the highest (219ft) and the heaviest (31 tons) ring of bells in the world. It also houses the world's largest organ, commissioned at a cost of £3,000,000. The organ, built by Henry Willis & Sons (as was the St. George's Hall organ) and Lewis & Co. Ltd has 145 speaking stops and nearly 10,000 separate pipes. One of the magnificent stained glass windows contains 18,000 square feet of glass, the spacious interior well capable of accommodating a congregation of 3000.

The Central Tower, called the Vesty Tower is 330 feet high but actually stands at 466 feet above sea level giving excellent views across the city and making it one of the largest Cathedrals in the world. This was Pope John Paul II's first port of call during his historic visit to Liverpool in May 1982. If you have ever wondered what the mini Greek Doric temple is on Upper Duke Street, this is the Mortuary Chapel which once oversaw the burials in the Cathedral grounds. Although of Gothic style, it is strongly marked with the individuality of the architect.

METROPOLITAN CATHEDRAL OF CHRIST THE KING:

It is viewed on a photograph here, taken from Mount Pleasant which was formerly Martindale Hill. The original attempt at this cathedral got under way in 1856 but stopped no sooner had it started. It was on 5th June 1933 that the foundations were laid on what was the site of the old workhouse. Six years later WWII blighted any further progress of the grand building that was to be housed here.

It was 1958 before it was decided that because of the elaborate design, there were not going to be enough funds to carry the project through and that modifications would have to be implemented. In 1959, Frederick Gibbert, a Protestant, designed what was to be the third attempt at the Catholic Cathedral. At this point, the underground crypt designed by Edwin Lutyens was already in place containing three chapels. The Chapel of Relics, Our Lady of Dolours and Crucifixion. In the former lies the body of Archbishop Whiteside.

Consecrated on the feast of Pentecost, Whit Sunday 14th May 1967,

it contains some of the finest modern stained glass windows in the country. The lantern tower contains 16 vertical windows and produces ever changing interior lighting and colour depending on the position of the sun in the sky. The crown of thorns are not only represented by the spiked roof but also by the shining metal tubes which hang beneath the central tower. The high altar is a 19 ton single slab of white marble shipped from Yugoslavia. Outwards from the altar is seating for 2,700 people. Outside the Cathedral are two concrete triangular structures encasing four bells named Matthew, Mark, Luke and John.

MYRTLE GARDENS:

One of the largest phases in the tenement scheme was Myrtle Gardens. Built in 1936, east of the city centre on the site of the old Liverpool orphanage. Consisting of 344 flats, less than fifty years later they were derelict. After being sold off to Barrett's, they were successfully converted to student accommodation and re-named Minster Court.

A little further east of these blocks on the periphery of the city centre stood tenement blocks behind Mason Street off Irvine Street to the

Myrtle Gardens enjoying a new lease of life as Minster Court, viewed from Melville Place.

rear of Paddington Comprehensive School and Cardwell Street off Smithdown Lane and on Crown Street. The former stood derelict for quite some time before the iron ball caught up with them in the late 1980s.

CHINA TOWN:

One single block in Nelson Street dating from the 1920s still exists today with the addition of a central stairway. It is adjoined to the 'Blackie' building on Gt George St which was built in 1840 in the heart of Liverpool's Chinatown which is the oldest Chinese community in Europe. The nearby Nook public house keeps tradition by calling time to its drinkers in Cantonese. Nearby, off the top of Duke Street runs Kent Street and Lydia Ann Street. Here stood Kent Gardens. Kent Street was named after William Kent, a wealthy merchant and ship owner who in 1768 built his residence there.

Nelson Street tenements in their 21st century guise.

Lydia Ann Street took its name from the wife of George Perry who was manager of the Phoenix Foundry which was at the end of the street. Merseyside's first marine engine was built there and a blue plaque commemorating the occasion took pride of place on the tenement wall. Cornwallis Street which runs south of these was named in commemoration of Charles, 1st Marquis Cornwallis, born in 1738. He was Governor of Ireland and India where he died in 1805. A salt water swimming baths once stood here. Nearby Frederick Street was where Liverpool legend Kitty Wilkinson founded the first washhouse in 1842, helping stem the tide of cholera epidemics which were sweeping the city in the 1830s.

TOXTETH AND DINGLE:

Stanhope House, off Upper Parliament Street took its name from nearby Stanhope and Upper Stanhope Street which were named after the Earl of Harrington which the area was once called. The 1st Earl of Sefton married Isobella Stanhope, the daughter of the Earl of Harrington. These blocks were in an advanced state of decay by the late 1980s, new flats now stand on Chesterfield Street.

Caryl Gardens, which covered the block next to the Royal Southern Hospital, incorporated seating areas, ornate lighting and a children's playground. Built in 1938, it was bounded by Hill, Grafton, Warwick and Caryl Streets, and served the Toxteth and Dingle communities well. Caryl Street took its name from the Molyneux family which owned most of Toxteth Park. Caryl was the 3rd Viscount Molyneux. Lord Street in the city centre was also named after him.

Warwick Gardens, also from 1938 was built partly on the old site of St. Thomas in the Fields Church on Warwick Street. Sussex Gardens and its annexe Sussex Gardens West which overlook Upper Warwick Street and Park Road were built somewhat later in the late 1940's due to the post war housing shortage and have been renovated and given a new lease of life. These were the last tenements to be built in the inter-war design as the Corporation policy in this era was to build three storey blocks of flats, the like of which sprouted up all over Liverpool in the late 1940s and 1950s. An example of this type was the previously mentioned Gerard Close, which completed the Gerard Crescent development somewhat later than the rest. Other tenements in the Toxteth area were St. James Gardens and Prince Albert Gardens from 1935 which were demolished in 1981 whilst nearby stood King Gardens.

1962 - An aerial view from the Anglican Cathedral showing Nelson Street tenements in the foreground. Beyond, off Kent Street lie Kent Gardens

Kent Gardens off Kent Street and Lydia Ann Street tinned up ready for demolition

FURTHER AFIELD:

Many other tenement blocks from the 1930s were built on the outskirts of the city centre. St. Oswald's Gardens on St. Oswald's Street in the Old Swan area of Liverpool were built on a curve running into Prescot Road. These housed a large row of shops beneath which served the Old Swan community into the 1990s. A Tesco superstore now sits on this site.

Stanhope House seen here from Upper Parliament Street. Derelict, their time has been and gone.

Wavertree High Street was also host to a block, which after extensive repair and alteration have become Abbeygate Apartments. A fine example of what could have been achieved with many more of these flats, given the number of apartments being built in the city centre to accommodate the ever growing student population.

Sussex gardens seen here from Upper Warwick Street. Although similar in design to the inter-war tenements, these particular blocks were built after WW II due to the housing shortage.

Dingle House and South Hill House at the Aigburth end of Park Road were early examples of these inter-war flats having been built in 1923. Even further south of the city centre in Garston were later blocks built on Speke Road.

CITY CENTRE LIVING: THE HIGH RISE FLATS

The next phase of building on a large scale wasn't until the mid 1950s and was inspired by the sky scrapers of New York. Land available for building was at a premium so multi-storey blocks of flats were deemed to be the way forward.

At first, residents were delighted with their new homes. Comfort, views, peace and quiet, and the sense of space were a novelty. However, it soon became apparent that the down side to this was people feeling isolated with few near neighbours, particularly when a lack of security led to vandalism of the lifts which left residents stranded. This rendered the blocks unsuitable for the elderly, the disabled or likewise, young families and as their novelty soon wore off, some of these blocks lasted even shorter than the housing built from the turn of the century. It is now nationally recognised that this type of housing was a huge mistake by the planners.

Coronation Court on the Sparrow Hall Estate off the East Lancashire Road was the first to be born out of this idea. Revolutionary methods of comfort and style could now be implemented, namely central heating and instant hot water. This block was demolished in 2002. Cresswell Mount, also completed in 1957 stood on top of Everton Ridge at St. George's Hill until its demolition in 1984.

By 1965 there were 79 blocks of multi-storey high rise buildings comprising 5,684 flats. By 1969 this had increased to 112 blocks. The first phase tended to be of a rectangular shape whereas those built square on were from the 1960s. There was also a fashion for these high rise flats to be built in groups of three, though it was not always the case.

Some examples of this were the Piggeries on William Henry Street, namely Crosbie, Canterbury and Haigh Heights (1958-80) as well as John F. Kennedy Heights (1964-99) on Everton Brow and Mazzini, Garibaldi and Cavour Heights(1960-88) to the north of Roscommon Street. Further afield, Sheil Park Heights on Sheil Road were another

1966 - William Henry Street shops (still there) looking up towards the Piggeries

group of three, namely Pendine, Kenley and Linosa and stood out as a landmark for many years until demolition of two of the blocks. On the East Lancashire Road at Croxteth stand the Altbridge Park trio and in Sefton Park we have Buckingham, York and Rutland House.

Other groups of three still to survive are Mosscraig, Firscraig and Whincraig as well as Tarncliff, Merecliff and Denecliff, the two groups being within a few hundred yards of each other in the Stockbridge Village area of Liverpool. In Huyton near the Bluebell estate are the three blocks of Wingate Towers, though these are now under demolition. In Seaforth we have Mongomery, Churchill and Alexander House.

Moving back to the Everton area, Candia and Crete Tower stood at the bottom of Everton Valley until a name change to Freedom Heights when sold off to a private developer a few years ago. Now they have a private car park and 24 hour security at their entrance. Nearby on Medea Street stood Medea Towers until its demolition in the 90s. Marwood Tower on nearby Boundary Street east still survive as does Corinth Tower a little further along Netherfield Road North, though this is scheduled for demolition. Most of the high rise in this area were demolished in recent years such as Edinburgh, Seacombe and Ellison Towers (another set of three) which came to their demise in 2002. St. George's Heights which stood further along Everton Ridge at Liverpool's highest point was demolished in June 2000, The famous Braddocks and Rock View were also wiped from the landscape during the same era but even until as recently as the early 1980s, nearly 20 high rise flats stood in the Netherfield Road area alone.

1966 - The children's playground at the junction of Great Homer Street and Kirkdale Road. Marwood Tower stands over it.

In 1993, Liverpool Housing Action Trust (HAT), took over the running of 67 of the remaining tower blocks and to date, many of these in Childwall, Storrington Heys and Sheil Park have since been demolished.

Brynford and Millburn Heights (1966) which stood on Conway Street running west from Netherfield Road to Great Homer Street fell into such a state of disrepair that in 1985, the Labour run Liverpool City Council sold them off to a private developer, Landmark, at 10p per flat. This was less expensive than maintenance, repair or even demolishing them.

Renamed as Landmark Towers and the Inn on the Park, asylum seekers of different nationalities took up residence in many of the flats in 2001. Living in squalor, their plight was only highlighted when they went on hunger strike and organisations which were sympathetic to their cause, went on demonstrations. Liverpool City Council re-housed them and a year later, Manchester Company LPG paid around one million pounds for both blocks, investing six million pounds in turning them into luxury apartments and penthouse suites.

A view along Netherfield Road North. many of these high rise including George's Heights have now gone

Renamed again, this time at View 146, apartments and suites ranging from 50K to £250,000 sold out within 24 hours of going on sale - a turnaround of a magnitude not seen before with this type of housing in Liverpool. With the building of the massive, privately owned Beetham Tower on Old Hall Street, and the plans for a £70M, 50 storey skyscraper at Brunswick Quay it seems there is a case for high rise living as long as it's done properly with security and maintenance.

John F Kennedy Heights from an Everton view point.

In the Vauxhall area off Fontenoy Street stand Adlington and Bispham House. Built in 1967 they are currently undergoing another spate of modernisation but at least still survive whilst similar blocks from that era on Tatlock Street and Blenheim Street were demolished in 1995. Over the bridge in the Athol Street area stood the white block of Logan Towers on Hedley Street. When built this was the world's tallest block of prefabricated flats at 22 storeys. New modern housing now occupies this site which was cleared in 1991. Higher up Boundary Street, which is the old Kirkdale boundary beyond Liverpool stood Sheehan Heights. These too were razed to the ground, the area now covered with new build housing.

Netherfield Road north towards Kirkdale Road. Most of this property has now gone

Trinity Vaults - Latimer Street, currently undergoing renovation. The high rise seen here are Sheehan Heights

Logan Towers from Shadwell Street. Merseyside Development Corporation and Liverpool Council together with associations such as Merseyside Improved Houses and Liverpool Housing Trust revitalised the area with around 500 new houses.

Titchfield Street/James Clarke Street seen from Green Street. Tatlock, Blenheim and Logan Towers are all in view.

Student Accommodation and Halls of Residence going up on Great Crosshall Street and Marybone.

I hope you have enjoyed this book and I welcome your feedback, positive or otherwise. I will be happy to answer any questions you may have via the Scottie Press websites forum on www.scottiepress.org.uk

I apologise if your particular place of interest was omitted but this could have been down to availablity in print or the sheer volume of photographs, which had to be whittled down to a sensible number.

Thank you,

Gerard Fagan.